DEFENDING OUR NATION

CITIZEN SOLDIERS

THE NATIONAL GUARD

Series Titles

DEFENDING OUR NATION

CITIZEN SOLDIERS
THE NATIONAL GUARD

FOREWORD BY
MANNY GOMEZ, ESQ., SECURITY AND TERRORISM EXPERT

BY
MICHAEL KERRIGAN

MASON CREST

Mason Crest
450 Parkway Drive, Suite D
Broomall, PA 19008
www.masoncrest.com

Printed in the United States of America
First printing
9 8 7 6 5 4 3 2 1

Series ISBN: 978-1-4222-3759-5
Hardcover ISBN: 978-1-4222-3760-1
ebook ISBN: 978-1-4222-8016-4

Library of Congress Cataloging-in-Publication Data

Names: Kerrigan, Michael, 1959- author.
Title: Citizen soldiers : the National Guard / FOREWORD BY MANNY GOMEZ, ESQ.,
 SECURITY AND TERRORISM EXPERT ; BY MICHAEL KERRIGAN.
Description: Broomall, Pennsylvania : MASON CREST, [2018] | Series: Defending our nation | Includes index.
Identifiers: LCCN 2016053128| ISBN 9781422237601 (hardback) | ISBN
 9781422237595 (series) | ISBN 9781422280164 (ebook)
Subjects: LCSH: United States--National Guard--Juvenile literature.
Classification: LCC UA42 .K442 2017 | DDC 355.3/70973--dc23

Developed and Produced by Print Matters Productions, Inc. (www.printmattersinc.com)
Cover and Interior Design by Bill Madrid, Madrid Design
Additional Text by Kelly Kagamas Tomkies

CONTENTS

KEY ICONS TO LOOK FOR:

Words to understand: These words with their easy-to-understand definitions will increase the reader's understanding of the text while building vocabulary skills.

Sidebars: This boxed material within the main text allows readers to build knowledge, gain insights, explore possibilities, and broaden their perspectives by weaving together additional information to provide realistic and holistic perspectives.

Educational Videos: Readers can view videos by scanning our QR codes, providing them with additional educational content to supplement the text. Examples include news coverage, moments in history, speeches, iconic sports moments and much more!

Text-dependent questions: These questions send the reader back to the text for more careful attention to the evidence presented there.

Research projects: Readers are pointed toward areas of further inquiry connected to each chapter. Suggestions are provided for projects that encourage deeper research and analysis.

Series glossary of key terms: This back-of-the-book glossary contains terminology used throughout this series. Words found here increase the reader's ability to read and comprehend higher-level books and articles in this field.

FOREWORD

VIGILANCE

We live in a world where we have to have a constant state of awareness—about our surroundings and who is around us. Law enforcement and the intelligence community cannot predict or stop the next terrorist attack alone. They need the citizenry of America, of the world, to act as a force multiplier in order to help deter, detect, and ultimately defeat a terrorist attack.

Technology is ever evolving and is a great weapon in the fight against terrorism. We have facial recognition, we have technology that is able to detect electronic communications through algorithms that may be related to terrorist activity—we also have drones that could spy on communities and bomb them without them ever knowing that a drone was there and with no cost of life to us.

But ultimately it's human intelligence and inside information that will help defeat a potential attack. It's people being aware of what's going on around them: if a family member, neighbor, coworker has suddenly changed in a manner where he or she is suddenly spouting violent anti-Western rhetoric or radical Islamic fundamentalism, those who notice it have a duty to report it to authorities so that they can do a proper investigation.

In turn, the trend since 9/11 has been for international communication as well as federal and local communication. Gone are the days when law enforcement or intelligence organizations kept information to themselves and didn't dare share it for fear that it might compromise the integrity of the information or for fear that the other organization would get equal credit. So the NYPD wouldn't tell anything to the FBI, the FBI wouldn't tell the CIA, and the CIA wouldn't tell the British counterintelligence agency, MI6, as an example. Improved as things are, we could do better.

We also have to improve global propaganda. Instead of dropping bombs, drop education on individuals who are even considering joining ISIS. Education is salvation. We have the greatest production means in the world through Hollywood and so on, so why don't we match ISIS materials? We tried it once but the government itself tried to produce it. This is something that should definitely be privatized. We also need to match the energy of cyber attackers—and we need savvy youth for that.

There are numerous ways that you could help in the fight against terror—joining law enforcement, the military, or not-for-profit organizations like the Peace Corps. If making the world a safer place appeals to you, draw on your particular strengths and put them to use where they are needed. But everybody should serve and be part of this global fight against terrorism in some small way. Certainly, everybody should be a part of the fight by simply being aware of their surroundings and knowing when something is not right and acting on that sense. In the investigation after most successful attacks, we know that somebody or some persons or people knew that there was something wrong with the person or persons who perpetrated the attack. Although it feels awkward to tell the authorities that you believe somebody is acting suspicious and may be a terrorist sympathizer or even a terrorist, we have a higher duty not only to society as a whole but to our family, friends, and ultimately ourselves to do something to ultimately stop the next attack.

It's not *if* there is going to be another attack, but where, when, and how. So being vigilant and being proactive are the orders of the day.

Manny Gomez, Esq.
President of MG Security Services,
Chairman of the National Law Enforcement Association,
former FBI Special Agent, U.S. Marine, and NYPD Sergeant

CHAPTER 1

"ALWAYS READY, ALWAYS THERE"

The U.S. National Guard was established in 1607. Several businesses have been known to honor National Guard officers on their products. Baker, Pleasants & Frayser of Richmond Virginia printed portraits of three officers on their tobacco labels.

The atrocities of September 11, 2001, took America completely by surprise. The attack was unique in its wanton murderousness and ruthless cunning. In more than 200 years of its history, the United States has been at war many times, but never before has it faced a foe that is so cynical.

An attack not on an army in the field but on the ordinary man and woman on the street, the terrorist outrages shattered the routine of what had dawned as an ordinary working day. The victims of the onslaught were regular travelers and flight crews, not military personnel; they were office workers, police, and firefighters, not soldiers. The war against terrorism that followed has seen U.S. forces in action in Afghanistan, Iraq, and beyond.

Yet many experts firmly believe that those best equipped to protect America are to be found closer to home. An enemy that seeks to strike at civilians in their homes and offices is, they argue, best resisted at the battlefront: in the small towns and city neighborhoods of the nation. It is ironic that, as America faces this new threat to its way of life, it should be finding a new appreciation of one of its oldest institutions, the National Guard.

The Guard and Reserve forces of the U.S. military are more integrated with their active-duty counterparts than ever before.

Words to Understand

Insurgents: Revolutionaries, protestors.

Militias: People trained like soldiers but who aren't in the military.

Sorties: Missions flown by a single plane.

Established at the Start

The U.S. National Guard is as old as America itself—**militias,** based on the English model, were established by the first settlers in Jamestown, VA, in 1607. These were raised among the community's menfolk to provide security against Native American attack, and from 1755 on, against encroachments by French forces on Britain's North American possessions. The British officers responsible for training these militias for the defense of what were still colonies belonging to the British Crown seethed about the "rascals" under their command. "The Americans," reported General Wolfe in the 18th century, "were the dirtiest most contemptible cowardly dogs that you can conceive. There is no depending on them in action." They were, he concluded, "rather an encumbrance than any real strength to an army." What he and his countrymen failed to appreciate was that the militiamen would show a loyalty to one another that they would never think of granting their colonial masters, and that when it came to defending their homes and families, they could be both disciplined and awesomely determined.

The British would finally find out the hard way just how badly they had underestimated their charges. The militias played a leading role in the great drama of the Revolutionary War. Massachusetts lawyer John Adams found a new vocation as a guerrilla leader, fashioning these small but tight-knit groups into a formidable force of **insurgents**. Ready to mobilize at a minute's notice, the Minutemen (as they came to be called) first faced the British regulars (or Redcoats) at Lexington, MA, in 1775. Militarily, this was nothing more than a skirmish, but it was a skirmish of enormous symbolic significance, and it was followed immediately by a more serious engagement at Concord. Here, to the amazement of all—not least, perhaps, of the ragtag army of the settlers themselves—a considerable British force was faced down and compelled to retreat in disgrace.

The English Militias

The English militias date back to medieval times, when people in the countryside were expected to serve their lords, not only with labor on the land but also with assistance as archers on the field of battle when required. This feudal system had died out by the 16th century, and the small farmer was no longer a bound serf but a freeborn yeoman. However, the view that there were tasks to be done for the nation still survived. The yeomanry, or militia, was organized at the local village, town, or county level, but it added up at the national level to a considerable and well-trained force.

Minutemen firing on the British in Massachusetts.

Farther south, in Virginia, the militias were organized by a wealthy planter, George Washington, who at first seemed destined to lead them into disaster and defeat. The rebels were holed up in Valley Forge, PA, northwest of Philadelphia, through the unforgiving winter of 1777–1778; they were apparently all but beaten by the cold and hunger. Under Washington's leadership, however, they found the character to emerge from that fearful ordeal with their heads unbowed.

Washington never forgot his militias. When he was eventually elected as the first president of the United States, he considered the militias to be crucial to the defense of the new republic. Their place in the U.S. Constitution was enshrined by the Founding Fathers, who gave the mi-

George Washington and his militia at Valley Forge.

litias the dual status still enjoyed by the National Guard. The National Guard is unique in that it is both a state and a federal organization. It is raised and organized by states to meet their own requirements. It is also federalized, which means that in times of national emergency it can be called upon by the U.S. government for the defense of America as a whole.

As such, the militias saw service throughout the 19th century, making a vital contribution, for instance, in the Mexican War of 1848. The acquisition of western territories, like California, New Mexico, and Utah, as well as that of Texas to the south, immediately transformed the United States in terms of size. However, the addition of Texas, in particular, served to extend and strengthen the slave-owning South, and thus to bring closer the agonizing conflict of the Civil War (1861–1865).

CURRIER,

an Army 4,500 men.
n Army 20,000 men.

BATTLE OF BUENA VISTA.

FOUGHT FEBY 23Yd 1847.

In which the American Army under Genl. Taylor were completely Victorious.

American Loss.— 272 Killed.
387 Wounded
6. Missing
Mexican Loss estimated in Killed
& Wounded.— 2000 men

On February 23, 1847, the Battle of Buena Vista took place under the command of Major General Zachary Taylor. The Americans were completely victorious.

As state fought state, the militias naturally played an important part, yet the struggle went right to the heart of their dual identity as members of a federal-state organization. The divisions were overcome, however, and the nation's National Guardsmen ended the century fighting together side by side to win victory in the Spanish-American War of 1898.

The American Spirit

The National Guard was always what we would now call a reservist force—part-time soldiers as opposed to a full-time standing army. Yet this did not for a moment mean it was unimportant. From the beginning, Americans were proud of their National Guard, feeling that in essential ways it embodied the national spirit. Whereas the standing armies of Europe were often instruments of oppression wielded by all-powerful monarchs, the National Guard represented democracy in action. The American citizen's right to bear arms had been enshrined by the U.S. Constitution of 1787—but it went hand in hand with a responsibility to bear them in defense of the country. George Washington was an early admirer of the militias, and Abraham Lincoln also prized them, considering them to be the essential and incorruptible protectors of his sacred goal of "government of the people, by the people, for the people."

So deeply was this principle etched into the U.S. identity that, for a long time, the country resisted the idea of having any sort of standing army at all. Times changed, however; in the late 19th and early 20th centuries, U.S. commitments overseas increased, and military technology grew in sophistication and complexity; the need for full-time specialist soldiers was now accepted. Accordingly, the regular army gained in importance; even so, its expansion was gradual. National Guard units represented 40 percent of U.S. forces in World War I (1914–1918) and were involved in every major action of World War II (1939–1945).

Into the Air

In World War I, new technologies posed new challenges. The strength of militias had previously lain in their amateurism—ordinary citizens standing shoulder to shoulder in defense of their homeland. Now, however, war had no place for unsophisticated soldiers. The potential costs of incompetence were just too great—for the soldiers, as well as for their comrades and country. Improved artillery, machine guns, gas, and tanks—such innovations transformed the face of frontline fighting. None, however, proved so significant as that of aviation.

It was reservists who led the way in the development of U.S. military aviation. The first planes to see action did so in what was seen as a secondary support role as "eyes in the sky." Between World War I and World War II, no fewer than 29 observation squadrons were set up—all under the command of the National Guard. As the importance of air power

Three Douglas O-46A and three North American O-47 aircraft assigned to the Maryland National Guard's 104th Observation Squadron conduct a training sortie in 1940.

became better appreciated, a designated U.S. Air Force slowly took shape, although it did not break free from the authority of the U.S. Army until 1947. A separate Air National Guard (ANG) was established at the same time. Its 58,000 personnel were divided among 84 fighter squadrons, and its primary role was the air defense of the continental United States.

The ANG was founded against the express wishes of many of the air chiefs, who believed that no part-time force could conceivably command the skills and experience necessary to wage war successfully in the air. In some cases, their fears were indeed well founded: many units, with obsolete aircraft and untrained fliers, proved a definite liability when called into action in Korea. Yet

What's in a Name?

The title "National Guard" was brought to America from revolutionary France by the idealistic young Marquis de Lafayette, a former commander of the Garde Nationale de France. A friend and protégé to Washington, Lafayette was also an inspiration to his older mentor, who admired the Frenchman's fierce love of freedom. Despite the most honorable of intentions, the French Revolution of 1789 quickly degenerated into wholesale tyranny and bloodshed.

America, accordingly, represented a "second chance" for the values of democracy. The name "National Guard" stood for America's rejection of foreign rule, its resolve to run its own affairs, and its determination to protect itself against outside enemies. The militias took up the title only gradually from 1824 onward. Not until 1900 was it recognized as the official name of the U.S. militias as a whole.

The Marquis de Lafayette at the naming of the National Guard.

others conducted themselves with great distinction—and in any case, where problems did arise, these were quite clearly the result of inept command and inadequate resourcing. As these lessons were learned and the problems addressed, the ANG gradually emerged as a well-equipped, skilled, and highly motivated fighting force. The value of its contribution in subsequent conflicts is not disputed—in the Vietnam War and the Gulf War, for instance, it did heroic service. In the Vietnam War, ANG squadrons flew 24,124 **sorties** and 38,614 combat hours. It is especially well suited to its current role in Operation Noble Eagle, which began minutes after the events of September 11 began and continue today, assuring the air defense of the American homeland.

Text-Dependent Questions

1. Why did militias first form in the early colonies?
2. What percentage of U.S. military forces in World War II did the National Guard represent?
3. What role did the National Guard play in creating an aviation military program?

Research Projects

1. The National Guard serves its state and the country as a whole. Select a time when the Guard was called to serve the entire country. Research to find out how many and which Guard units met the call and how long their mission lasted.
2. Research Operation Noble Eagle. Describe its mission, what National Guard units have been involved and when, and how successful this operation has been.

CHAPTER 2

THE NATIONAL GUARD TODAY

Private First Class Carla Shull receiving her Missouri National Guard Panama Service Ribbon after she and other members from the 1138th Military Police Company returned home from Operation Just Cause.

Now, as throughout its history, the National Guard stands at the center of American life, the first line of defense for those democratic freedoms the United States holds dear. The world's greatest democracy is protected, today, as in the 18th century, by a body of part-time, yet wholly committed, citizen-soldiers.

Their motivation is simple: they are defending their own communities and their own homes and families. This also earns them the respect of their fellow Americans. Washington, D.C., may be a distant city; the regular Army and Air Force may seem remote—yet the National Guard is never more than a few blocks away. A friend in need, it has assisted not only in times of war, but also in times of natural disasters and civic disorder, touching the lives of countless citizens across America.

For a long time, the National Guard was afflicted by those same problems of racism and sexism that bedeviled U.S. society as a whole. It was quick, however, in recognizing these evils to be themselves a threat to America's most vital freedoms. And in recent decades, the National Guard has worked vigorously to ensure that it is truly representative of all Americans, men and women, regardless of their color or their religious or cultural background.

A Dual Structure

As it is organized today, the National Guard is a reservist reflection of the United States' regular forces, closely resembling those services in everything from staffing structures to equipment

Words to Understand

Adjutant general: Chief administrative officer.

Deploy: Organize and send out.

Grassroots: Basic, at lowest level.

and training. Unlike the Army and Air Force, however, the National Guard units are organized by state, and in normal circumstances are answerable first and foremost to their state governors. Administratively speaking, therefore, the National Guard leads something of a "double life," under the dual control of both state and national military structures.

A National Guard Helicopter drops water on a Cold Spring Fire. Nearly 75 Colorado Guard members were called in to help and assist with the fire.

At the state level, an **adjutant general** is responsible for running the organization from day to day, and for commanding National Guard units on the ground under active duty. Career soldiers and air force officers, these men and women are an integrated part of the overall structure of the U.S. military. They are, therefore, under the administrative authority of the directors of the Army and Air National Guards and the umbrella organization of the National Guard Bureau (NGB). These report, in turn, to the secretaries of the Army and Air Force, and through them to the Secretary of Defense—and to the President, as Commander in Chief.

Only in times of war or national emergency, however, may the President order the National Guard into action. In other circumstances, it remains under the direction of state governors, who may call for its help in dealing with any natural disasters or civil disorders that may arise. Either way, it is commanded on the ground by military officers and may be **deployed** only on the decision of elected officials; the democratic basis of the organization is never to be forgotten. The respect in which the National Guard has been held has always depended on its being seen as a force for democracy, not only accountable to, but in a profound sense belonging to, the American people.

First Reserves

The significance of the U.S. National Guard can be difficult for people outside America to grasp. Elsewhere in the world, reservist forces tend, quite literally, to be held in reserve, playing a strictly secondary, subordinate role to the "real" regular armed services. No such distinction is made in the United States. The National Guard is by any standards a substantial and formidable military force. The Army National Guard has well more than 400,000 members, the Air National Guard around 120,000, and both are equipped to the same standards as the regular armed forces. Units are to be found in all 50 states, as well as in the Commonwealth of Puerto Rico, the territories of Guam and the Virgin Islands, and the District of Columbia.

Levels of fitness and training are just as exacting. No special or exceptional allowances are made for the fact that these are only part-time personnel, because these men and women will fight alongside their comrades in the regular forces on equal terms. Those enlisting in the

The Ohio Army National Guard participates in a two-week training course with the Army infantry.

National Guard know they will be expected to start by serving for six months on active duty with the regular Army or Air Force to achieve a basic grounding in the skills required, and that thereafter they will have to dedicate a minimum of 38 full days a year to training.

In order to rise through the ranks, they will have to match the abilities and expertise of full-time Army and Air Force officers. If anything, the standards are still higher: men and women of the National Guard certainly have a wider range of skills to master than their counterparts in the regular forces. They will routinely be called on to deal not only with outbreaks of war around the world but also with a range of domestic situations, from inner-city rioting to floods, from forest fires to nuclear incidents, and chemical spills.

Members of the Texas National Guard were called in to assist residents in Wharton, TX, after severe flooding. Members helped stranded residents make their way to rescue vehicles and personnel.

For All Americans

A guard, not only against the sort of military threats originally envisaged but against all manner of environmental disasters and civil disturbances, the National Guard has interpreted its defensive mission ever more widely over time. In recent decades, it has also reexamined what is meant by the word "National" in its name. As with other U.S. institutions, the National Guard for a long time contented itself with representing an America of white males. The idea that women or members of other ethnic communities might have a part to play was dismissed—if, indeed, it occurred at all.

American society has been changing, however. Compared with its predecessor of 10 years before, Census 2000 showed a 58 percent rise in America's Hispanic population alone. From 2000 to 2010, the percent rise in Hispanic population was 43 percent. The number of non-Hispanic blacks was found to have risen by 21 percent in the same period, while there was a staggering 71 percent increase in the Asian American population (which increased by another 43 percent between 2000 and 2010). Although striking, these figures barely do justice to the

The Maryland National Guard was called in for the first time since 1968 to assist with peacekeeping operations in Baltimore after the death of an unarmed black man by police sparked outrage and protests.

scale of the transformation, for America's minorities have grown not only in size, but also in vociferousness.

In recent years, ethnic groups have been lobbying with growing confidence for their contributions to be recognized, their problems addressed, and their voices heard. The institutions of a democratic country have had to adapt to these changing circumstances, and the National Guard has led the way in opening up to the members of this more widely, multiracially defined American nation. Its leadership recognizes that the very legitimacy of the National Guard rests on its strong community base, its roots at once in national patriotism and **grassroots** neighborliness. A uniformly white, male, middle-class organization can make no claims to represent America today; an organization that discriminates against women and African, Hispanic, or Asian Americans can hardly expect to be regarded as a truly "National" Guard.

Today, 25.6 percent of Army National Guard members represent minority communities, while 10.5 percent of the members are now women. In the Air National Guard, 20.3 percent of the members come from ethnic minority groups, while 18.7 percent are women, according to a 2014 report published by the Department of Defense.

Now fully open and committed to members of all ethnic groups and to women, the National Guard has also been working hard to make itself accessible to disabled Americans, for they too have their own contribution to make and their inalienable right to make it. Efforts to accommodate these and other minorities may involve such basic steps as the installation of elevators and wheelchair ramps or—perhaps more crucial—the education of personnel and the imaginative reinterpretation of established procedures. In September 2011, the U.S. military, including the National Guard, lifted its ban against accepting openly gay and lesbian people, making it a truly representative organization of people of all ethnicities, genders, and sexual orientations.

In addition to accepting all ethnicities, genders, and sexual orientations, the Defense Department has opened up more combat roles for qualified women.

Switzerland's Weekend Soldiers

Famous as the home of the International Red Cross and sponsor of the Geneva Convention (the treaty governing the ethical conduct of conflict worldwide), Switzerland was a nonparticipant in the 20th century's two world wars—yet its fiercely guarded neutrality should not be confused with a lack of patriotism. Indeed, Switzerland can be seen as the world's most militarized democracy, its defensive system recalling the early American militia model in intriguing ways. Switzerland has no regular army as such, but every able-bodied male in the country between the ages of 20 and 42 must make himself available for regular training and military service for several weeks a year. In between times, he is bound by law to keep in practice on local rifle ranges and to keep a gas mask, weapons, and ammunition at home in readiness for potential emergencies.

Profile of a female airman in the Air National Guard.

Members of the Alaska Air National Guard and California Air National Guard participate in a mass-casualty training exercise.

A Woman's Place

When established in 1947, the National Guard had no place for women at any rank, nor was there any immediate prospect of a change in policy. Due to its peculiar dual identity as a state and federal organization, there was no single, central authority in a position to push through the necessary modernizations. By the mid-1950s, however, some Air Guard commanders were beginning to increase the number of females in their medical teams by bringing in nurses from the Air Force Reserve. To all intents and purposes, these women were serving as signed-up members of the National Guard. The moment the Guard was deployed, however, they were compelled to withdraw immediately, an absurd situation that served neither the National Guard units involved nor the women themselves.

In 1956, accordingly, Congress passed legislation permitting women to serve in the National Guard. The first to be appointed, Norma Pearsons, was assigned to the Air Guard's 106th Tactical Hospital. Soon there was a second woman, the Army Guard's first female officer, First Lieutenant Sylvia Marie St. Charles Law, who was commissioned in January 1957.

By the 1960s, many women were serving in both arms of the National Guard, although the reality was that they still represented only a tiny fraction of the total force. And vital as their contribution was, they were still confined to the relatively restricted sphere of military medicine. Through the 1970s, however, women succeeded in entering other areas of **rear-echelon** support: maintaining aircraft, driving trucks and heavy earth-moving equipment, as well as all manner of headquarters work.

Martha Rainville (center) in her role as a Federal Emergency Management Agency (FEMA) case studies specialist.

In 1989, Private First Class Charla Shull of the Missouri National Guard's 138th Military Police Company became the first guardswoman to come under fire when her unit was attacked in Panama by an enemy mortar. By 1991, however, a number of guardswomen were fighting in the Gulf War frontline, flying fighter jets and helicopters into the thick of the combat. By 1997, Lieutenant Colonel Martha Rainville had made history by becoming the first woman adjutant general (for the state of Vermont), and almost 40,000 women represented some 10 percent of the entire National Guard. As of 2014, women made up 18.8 percent of the National Guard, and 19 percent of its officers were women. And in 2016, Spc. Rachel Mayhew became Texas Army Guard's first female combat engineer.

Text-Dependent Questions

1. What government authority do National Guard units answer to?
2. When a person enlists in the National Guard how many months of active duty and how many days of training will he or she receive?
3. Who was the first woman to serve in the National Guard and what was her role with the Guard?

Research Projects

1. Research what the training program is like for National Guard enlistees. What does the training involve and how many enlistees drop out?
2. Research the life of Lt. Col. Martha Rainville. Include where she was born, her education and experience prior to joining the National Guard, and her career achievements while in the National Guard.

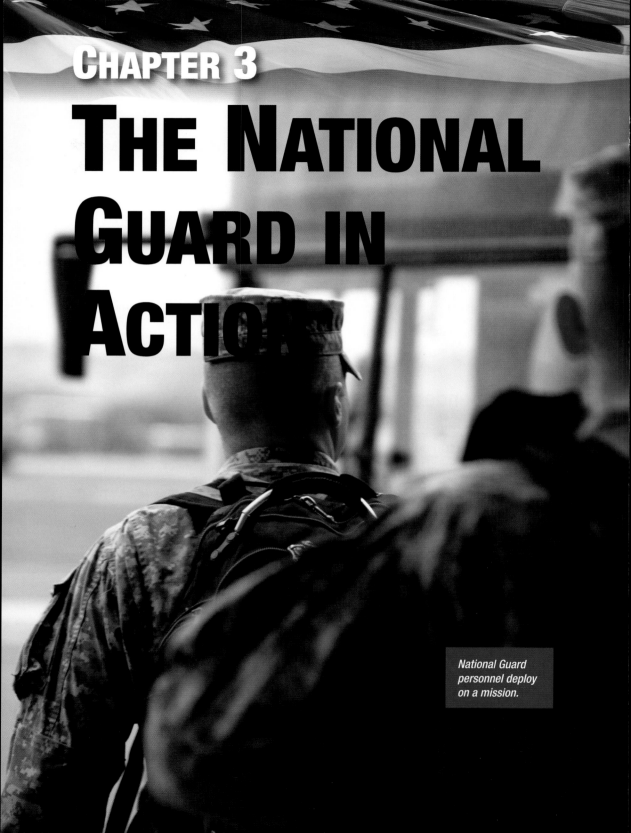

CHAPTER 3

THE NATIONAL GUARD IN ACTION

National Guard personnel deploy on a mission.

Rooted though it may be in community spirit and neighborly values, the National Guard has never been narrow in its outlook or restricted in its enterprise. Its mission to protect the American homeland has taken it all over the world in recent times.

From Korea and Vietnam, to Grenada and Panama, from Kuwait to Kosovo and Kabul—wherever Americans have fought since World War II, the National Guard has been there. In a rapidly shrinking world, America's frontiers have had to be defended at some distance; for several decades, the primary danger to freedom and international stability came from Communism. That threat was finally brought to an end by the collapse of the Soviet Union in 1989, but it would be followed by a succession of other menaces, ranging from South American **narcoterrorism** to Serbian nationalism in the Balkan region of southeastern Europe.

Recently, the forces of Islamic fundamentalism have posed the greatest hazard to peace and freedom in the world. Whatever the enemy, whatever the war, the National Guard has always been in the forefront of the action, its battle honors a match for those of any branch of the regular armed forces.

Korea

On June 25, 1950, the forces of Communist North Korea streamed across the 38th parallel in a wholesale invasion of South Korea, and America lost no time in going to the assistance of the beleaguered democracy. Beyond his concern for a country under assault from an armed aggressor, President Truman was motivated by his sense that, if America did not move to

Words to Understand

Fiasco: Total failure.

Narcoterrorism: Terrorism related to illegal drug trade.

Sovereign: Country or territory governed by one organized government.

meet what appeared to be a clear challenge, there might be no end to Communist expansion throughout the developing world. What was at first envisaged as a strictly limited intervention had to be scaled up radically in the following weeks, for American and South Korean troops met with a series of reversals. In October, just as the United States and its UN allies began to make progress, China entered the war. U.S. forces were thrown back in complete confusion after one of the worst defeats ever suffered by the American military. Both sides now dug in for a hard job, which recalled the trench-bound stalemates of World War I. More than 138,000 members of the Army National Guard served in Korea. Many were decorated for their bravery, and many hundreds were killed before South Korea could be liberated and democratic rule restored.

In July 1950, hundreds of Army and Air National Guard units were deployed, including the 40th Infantry Division of the California National Guard, to assist with the war in Korea.

Conflict and Challenge during the Korean War

One conflict that occurred during the Korean War was an internal one for the National Guard. During the Korean War, African Americans fought for their country—but not alongside their white compatriots. "We were segregated," recalls Lloyd Smith, who was a teenager when he left Washington, D.C., for Korea with the National Guard's 715th Transportation Truck Company. "D.C. was still segregated. The enlisted clubs were segregated. Everything was segregated." The enemy, however, did not discriminate, nor did the Korean winter: "They had snipers around. We were sleeping outside on the ground in sleeping bags. It was so cold, minus 30 degrees F [−35°C]. The Chinese were all over the place, dead. You'd wake up and the bag would be stuck to your face." Smith saw distinguished service, earning three Battle Stars to go with his Korean War Service medal, but never the right to equal consideration with his white comrades. "We were still segregated when we came back on ship. . . . We came back to Camp Stoneman, San Francisco, and they wouldn't let us go into town." Yet what he says about the National Guard is this: "It was an exercise in self-discipline . . . [which] calmed me down." Such ungrudging service from Lloyd Smith, and so many like him, would eventually help to change the National Guard.

While the Army National Guard (ANG) experienced its challenges, like segregation, during the Korean War, the Air Guard also faced a harrowing ordeal during the war, in the course of which the gravest shortcomings were highlighted. Obsolete aircraft were only part of the problem: pilots and crew were often utterly unprepared for combat, while organizational inadequacies meant the misallocation of such skills and resources the ANG was able to command. Matters were not helped, meanwhile, by the regular Air Force's habit of helping itself to essential equipment and key personnel as required, leaving ANG squadrons dangerously exposed.

As the war went on, however, the Air Guard slowly and painfully began to pick itself up, address its failings, and repair its reputation. In the end, its members went on to make a significant contribution to the overall American effort, flying 39,530 combat sorties in all. By the time the war was over, they had dropped 44,000 bombs and fired off 31,000 rockets and more than 16 million rounds of ammunition. More than 100 Air Guardsmen had been killed or reported missing in action, but the ANG could claim to have done important work in disrupting enemy communications and supply lines and hindering troop movements. Some 39 enemy planes had been downed and another 149 damaged—an impressive strike rate after such an unpromising start.

The Jet Set

Dick Mischke, now retired, served as an Air Guardsman in the Korean War, one of the first pilots trained to fly jet aircraft. "Our wing's assignment was interdiction," he recalls. "We provided air-to-ground combat support to Army ground troops. We dive-bombed, strafed, and dropped both aerial and napalm rockets. Most of our work dealt with dive-bombing the railroad tracks to cut off supply lines to enemy troops. We would also bomb warehouses, trucks, and tanks that we knew were supplying the North Koreans."

Mischke remembers vividly the day in 1951 when he took part in an attack on the main airport in North Korea's capital, Pyongyang. "It would be like bombing the National Airport in Washington, D.C. The entire wing—what was left of it, since we'd been losing pilots and aircraft all along—consisted of about 24 planes that went up and encountered a lot of MiGs [Soviet-built jet fighters]. We dive-bombed the runways so that the enemy aircraft couldn't use them. The antiaircraft fire was extremely intense, and the MiGs were all over us like mosquitoes."

The Air Guard's early fiasco can be seen in hindsight as having been a timely warning to the government and military. Work would continue throughout the 1950s to build upon the progress made in the course of the Korean War and to ensure that the humiliations the organization had suffered would never be repeated.

Inside the Air National Guard.

Vietnam

Korea had been the first major flare-up of what was to be a far more protracted confrontation, that long standoff between the Western democracies and the forces of global Communism known as the Cold War. Although outright hostilities never actually broke out between the United States and the Soviet Union, the superpowers came into conflict indirectly through a series of "proxy wars." Vietnam (1964–1974) was a case in point, with the Communist North, under the leadership of Ho Chi Minh, being a "client state," or "satellite," of the Soviet Union, while the South inevitably looked to the United States for support.

Where Korea had involved a tactically straightforward situation—the invasion of a country by an outside aggressor—the picture in Vietnam was more confused. Here, while there was a clear enough external enemy in the shape of the Northern forces, there were also Viet Cong in-

On May 13, 1968, 12,234 Army National Guardsmen in 20 units from 17 states were mobilized for service during the Vietnam War. Eight units deployed to Vietnam, and over 7,000 Army Guardsmen served in the war zone. Company D (Ranger), 151st Infantry, Indiana Army National Guard arrived in Vietnam in December 1968.

surgents in the South itself, fighting on behalf of—and with the active assistance of—the North. A loose confederation of guerrillas, without uniforms but with sophisticated Soviet weaponry at their command, they could strike at a moment's notice, and then simply melt away into the peaceful population. The American military was geared up to wage conventional war, winning set-piece battles through overwhelming force, and it found itself ill equipped to deal with so elusive and resilient an enemy. The more aggressively U.S. forces attempted to run the Viet Cong guerrillas to earth, the greater the risk that their actions would be attended by civilian casualties.

In the end, despite the fact that U.S. forces served with honor in Vietnam, the experience was finally to prove frustrating and even demoralizing for them. The sense that many at home opposed the war only added to their exasperation. The entire episode of the Vietnam War triggered a major crisis of confidence in the American military—indeed, in America as a whole.

The Army National Guard, which had been well represented on the ground in Vietnam, shared in the general mood of depression. Ready to fight for freedom, its members had found themselves trapped in an untenable position. Yet, in some respects, those who served within the United States had the harder time. Many guardsmen and -women found themselves on an increasingly fraught frontline at home, forced to maintain order on streets and college campuses in a time of widespread and ugly civil conflict between Viet Nam war protestors and law enforcement and military authorities.

For the Air Guard, Vietnam was a more positive experience. The ANG's spirits were lifted by the fact that, in meeting its first challenge since Korea, it was able to pass the test with flying colors.

The legion of the brave: the Kentucky National Guard in the Vietnam War.

End of the Cold War

The Cold War came closer to home at the end of 1979, when the pro-Communist politician Maurice Bishop seized power on the Caribbean island of Grenada. Of course, there had already been a Communist presence in the region for 20 years, ever since Fidel Castro's forces had taken power in Cuba, but this new development seemed to signal an escalation of the problem. Even so, the United States stood by, preferring not to interfere in the internal affairs of a **sovereign** country.

Such a detached position became increasingly difficult to maintain as time went by. As tensions within Bishop's government reached a breaking point, ending in the assassination of Bishop himself, there was a breakdown in civil order that threatened to deepen and spread. Given that this would endanger the lives of American medical students working on the island, the United States was left with little choice but to send in its forces to assure their safety and restore civil stability for the Grenadians at large. Many National Guard units participated in Operation Urgent Fury, which encountered greater-than-expected resistance but nonetheless succeeded in restoring order and democracy within months.

To a certain extent, Operation Just Cause in Panama, some six years later, was comparable. Again, the United States had been uneasy for some time with the rule of Panama's dictator, General Manuel Noriega, who had been **indicted** in America on drug trafficking charges. Yet only when law and order appeared to be breaking down, and the threat to U.S. nationals living and working in Panama appeared to be growing, did President George H. W. Bush decide that armed intervention was required. Again, many state National Guards were federalized for

Threats of Soviet nuclear bombers were everyone's concern, including the National Guard, for many years. For the first time in 1954, thousands of Army Guardsmen manned antiaircraft artillery positions across the country—the Guard's first federal mission while in state status.

the action and went on to play an important part in the restoration of a legitimate government in Panama. Guardsmen and -women served both in frontline engagement and in rear-echelon work, ensuring supplies, while National Guard military police units from across America assisted in reestablishing order and reassuring a terrified Panamanian population.

Blessed Are the Peacemakers

The happy conclusion of the Cold War did not bring all conflict to an end. Indeed, the collapse of the Soviet Union left a significant power vacuum in the world. Nowhere was this more clear than in the Balkans region of eastern Europe, where the former Communist state of Yugoslavia began to disintegrate amid scenes of spiraling ethnic violence. Although the iron grip of Communism on the country had left little room for individual freedom, it had also held the region's many ancient and bitter ethnic rivalries in check.

Once that grip had been removed, interethnic violence quickly flared as Serbia, the largest and most powerful regional state, embarked on a ruthless campaign of conquest to bring the whole of former Yugoslavia under Serbian rule. The UN and **NATO** forces eventually brought peace to the region—although not before countless lives had been lost through horrific programs of "ethnic cleansing." Nobody had any illusions about the uneasy stability that followed. Peacekeeping forces from around the world were brought in to ensure the safety of the region's many thousands of refugees.

The National Guard played their part as well. The experience of the West Texas National Guard is typical. In their six-month stint, they helped organize the safe return to their former homes of more than 8,000 families who had been displaced by the conflict. Under their supervision, meanwhile, more than 223,652 square yards (187,000 square meters) of fields, roadsides, and playgrounds were de-mined; half a million rounds of ammunition, 11,000 weapons, and six tons of high explosives were collected and safely destroyed. Any one of these mines or rifle rounds might have meant a life lost, a family bereaved. One officer summed it up simply: "We are leaving Bosnia a safer place than we found it."

The Gulf War

In the deserts of the Middle East, the Gulf War (1990–1991) represented something of a departure for the U.S. military. Saddam Hussein's invasion of Kuwait was an act of international piracy that threatened to upset the fragile balance of power in a region that supplied fully one-third of the world's oil production. It also left one of America's closest allies, Israel, dangerously vulnerable. Quick as ever to heed the call, the National Guard was soon shipping out to Saudi Arabia, where a massive force was being mustered in readiness to throw back the Iraqi aggressor. More than 75,000 of the Air and Army National Guard were involved, medical and trans-

Members of Company C, 3rd Battalion, 116th Infantry on guard at the Sava River in Bosnia.

Members of the Iowa National Guard take part in a medevac training exercise.

portation units, as well as frontline personnel, all playing their part in one of the largest-scale military operations the world has ever seen. Never far from the action once Operation Desert Storm began, the National Guard inevitably suffered casualties: in one instance, three members of the Californian National Guard's 126th Medical Company died when their helicopter crashed during a hazardous nighttime medevac (medical evacuation) mission.

They Also Serve

For every guardsman or -woman who serves, several other Americans may also be enlisted in the cause—those family members who stand by them in thick and thin, giving all their support. Speaking to a reporter from the *Reporter-News* of Abilene, West Texas, Leslie Ybarra said she had not realized how much she would miss her husband, Rick, when he left for Bosnia to serve along with other U.S. troops on the NATO peacekeeping force. This was not just a matter of missing him, she said. She had found his absence a trial in all sorts of little ways, from running the house to walking the dog and attending nursing school. "It's going to be so nice to have him here," she said, as news came through of his return. "I didn't want him to go, but I knew it would be best if he went."

Many thousands of refugee families in Bosnia will surely be glad that he did. Guardsmen and -women helped supervise the rebuilding of that country after its hideously destructive civil war. Rick waited until his return to tell Leslie about the continuing dangers he had faced from land mines around the guardsmen's base, concerned that it might have worried her to know.

Rick's comrade in the West Texas National Guard, Captain Greg Chaney, found a novel way of staying in touch with his daughters, Chelsea (age 8) and Chera (age 6). He recorded a series of bedtime stories for them in the weeks before he went. They had not wanted him to go, but they had understood when he told them he was going to help other little girls get back to their homes. Even so, said mother Angie, they had frequently cried themselves to sleep. Now that he was home, however, they felt nothing but joy and pride.

Text-Dependent Questions

1. What event led to the United States' involvement in the Korean War?
2. Name at least two problems the Air National Guard experienced during the Korean War.
3. What was the National Guard's role in Operation Just Cause in Panama?

Research Projects

1. Research the history behind the conflict between Serbia and Yugoslavia. What led up to the UN and NATO deploying peacekeeping forces?
2. Research the National Guard's role in Operation Desert Storm. How many units were involved? Over what period of time? How many casualties were there?

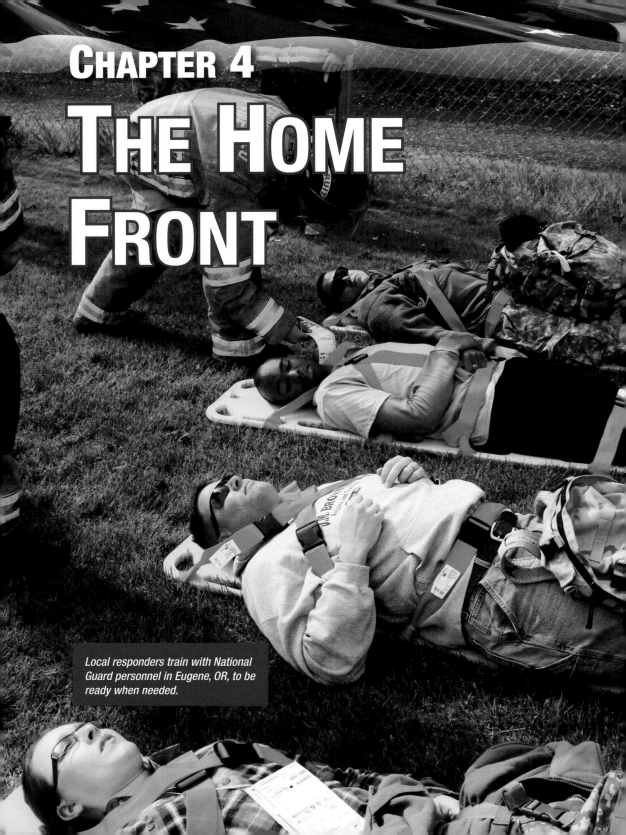

CHAPTER 4
THE HOME FRONT

Local responders train with National Guard personnel in Eugene, OR, to be ready when needed.

The terrorist attacks on the World Trade Center and the Pentagon on September 11, 2001, left many Americans with an unaccustomed sense of vulnerability. No one could recall a time in which the American homeland had seemed so imminently under threat.

Despite 200 years of history, during which America's armed forces had fought in many conflicts beyond the boundaries of the United States, there seemed to be no precedent for so direct a danger. The National Guard, however, knew otherwise. It had been established at a time when the first settlers lived in daily risk of attack, and the militias had come of age in armed struggles, first against the French, and afterward against their own British colonial overlords.

Moreover, it may be true that no nation had dared since then to attack Americans in their homeland, but Mother Nature had shown no such reluctance: the National Guard were well used to meeting the threats posed by floods and fires and other such disasters. To come to their country's aid in its moment of adversity was thus the first instinct of America's guardsmen and -women. Moreover, the expertise and experience they had gained down through the decades stood them in good stead in this time of crisis. Countless Americans have told of the profound sense of gratitude and reassurance they felt on seeing the National Guard patrolling their streets—but to the guards themselves, it was nothing more than business as usual.

Words to Understand

Accumulated: Gathered together.

Extremist: One who holds extreme political or religious views.

Unprecedented: Not having been done before.

Georgia Army National Guard Soldiers fill sand bags in anticipation of possible flooding. More than 200 Guardsmen, State Defense Force Volunteers and Youth Challenge Academy Graduates filled 8,000 sand bags for use in Georgia and South Carolina.

Standing Guard

In an order on September 14, 2001, President George W. Bush announced the call-up of some 50,000 National Guard and other reservist troops, federalized for a period of up to two full years. Although there had been other mass mobilizations, most recently in 1991 for Operation Desert Storm, this was the biggest call-up in a domestic crisis since 1916, when President Woodrow Wilson had sought to seal off the entire southern border after a raid on Columbus, NM, by the notorious brigand Pancho Villa.

Arkansas Army National Guard during Desert Storm.

President Bush's step was a drastic one, but this was a dramatic situation. Guardsmen and -women were in no doubt as to where their duty lay. "We're behind the President," said New York Army Guard Sergeant 1st Class Larry Signer when he heard the order. "Not one Guard soldier is complaining about anything they have to do." A resident of upstate New York, Sergeant Signer had already been on duty for some days in the aftermath of the attack on the World Trade Center and was deeply angered at an assault on what he felt was practically his home city. "We're taking this personally," said another guardsman, Sergeant David Perez, interviewed as he worked among the rubble of Ground Zero; his 1st Battalion, 69th Infantry Unit, was Manhattan based.

Arkansas Army National Guard during Desert Storm.

"America the Vulnerable"

In the weeks following the September 11, 2001, attacks, Americans witnessed an **unprecedented** tightening of security measures in every area of life as authorities reacted to a situation that nobody had seriously anticipated. Since the collapse of the Soviet Union in 1989, America had been unrivaled as both an economic and a military superpower; its citizens had grown accustomed to the feeling that they were essentially invulnerable. In the area of airport security, for example, such efforts that were made pre-September 11 had tended to be half-hearted; the traveling public had not proved tolerant when it came to flight delays. The assault by Islamic **extremist** Al Qaeda terrorists changed all that. Suddenly sensing that they were under attack, Americans accepted the authorities' attempts to stiffen what had often been the slackest of procedures.

Terrorism had for years been a fact of life in a country such as Israel, whose citizens had learned to put up with security measures that most Americans would resent as intrusive, just as British and Spanish citizens had learned vigilance through years of atrocities by Irish and Basque separatist terrorist groups. With the attacks of September 11, 2001, it became clear that Americans, too, would have to acquire these instincts in a hurry—and despite the efforts made in the immediate aftermath of the attacks, it is also clear that there is much to learn.

Many commentators have sneered that the assignment of National Guard units to duties in public buildings and on airport security has had more effect in boosting morale than in actually countering terrorism, and the charge would appear to be true, as far as it goes. In a sphere where they are as yet inexperienced, the guardsmen and -women may have much to learn, but there can be no doubt, either, that they have an inestimable contribution to make to the protection of Americans in the coming years. As the nation faces an enemy that aims to strike in its cities, in its workplaces and homes, who could be better placed to spearhead the resistance than the National Guard? With an all-American patriotism balanced by strong roots in local communities, the National Guard is uniquely equipped to foster the sort of street-level vigilance that will be required from now on.

Doing Their Duty

On the morning of Tuesday, September 11, 2001, a hijacked airliner smashed into the Pentagon, turning one side of the building into an inferno. National Guard units were among those called in to help. Rescuers formed human chains, from 8 to 10 people long, stretching as far as they could into the building where toxic, black smoke billowed as debris fell from walls and ceilings.

Undeterred by the searing heat, two Army National Guard medical soldiers, Major Gary McKay and Master Sergeant James Smith, crawled low along corridors, snatching their breaths through water-soaked T-shirts. "It's lucky we were at the right place at the right time to help other people," said Smith. "We saw people running down the hall, lights going off, and we decided we needed to do something."

They remember feeling anxious only at one point—when a report came that another hijacked plane might come crashing into the Pentagon in a matter of minutes. Thankfully, it proved wrong, and the rescue work continued. In the best traditions of the National Guard, the two men make reluctant heroes: "People wearing every color of uniform came together and did what they had to do," was all Smith would say.

A North Dakota Air National Guard F-16 on a combat air patrol over the Pentagon on September 11, 2001, after the hijacked American Airlines Flight 77 crashed into it.

Enemy Fire

The ability of the National Guard to organize successfully in dealing with domestic disasters is encouraging. The National Guard has skills that have been perfected through many decades of coping with calamities and crises of every sort. The Louisiana National Guard, for instance, is as proud of its work after the great Mississippi River floods of the 1920s as it is of its valiant

The great Mississippi River flood of 1927 was one of the worst natural disasters in American History. Although National Guard aviation units had been regularly called upon to assist civil authorities since early in that decade, the 1927 flood marked the first time that an entire Guard flying unit and its government-issued aircraft had been mobilized to help deal with a major natural disaster.

service in America's wars. The former chief of the National Guard Bureau, Army Lt. Gen. H. Steven Blum, called the National Guard's response to Hurricane Katrina the finest hour in its 400-year history. More than 50,000 guardsmen and -women assisted in search and rescue, medical treatment, evacuation, and security when the hurricane struck on August 29, 2005.

In 1998, when an abnormally rainless summer left woodlands and even swamps in Florida kindling-dry, the state's National Guard found themselves in the front line against a ferocious enemy—fire.

After the "Holiday Fire" of Memorial Day, May 25, 1998, a series of blazes swept the state's northern interior, destroying huge stands of timber, jeopardizing the environment, and threatening hundreds of homes. Around 1,800 Guard troops were rushed in from Florida and from neighboring Georgia. They brought with them Kiowa, Black Hawk, and Chinook helicopters, as well as water tankers and heavy earth-moving equipment.

The first task was containment. Guardsmen bulldozed their way through brush and woodland in the path of the advancing fire-front. Others followed, damping down the ground to make what they hoped would be an effective fuel-free barrier against the oncoming flames. Their efforts were guided by members of the state Air Guard, who overflew the infernos in their C-26 observation planes, using infrared cameras to pinpoint "hotspots" for firefighters working on the ground. While soldiers on the ground struggled to clear firebreaks, their comrades made countless airborne passes in helicopters, dropping huge quantities of water in the hopes of dousing, or at least suppressing, the worst of the blaze. Between June 8 and July 7, Black Hawk crews dropped 1.4 million gallons of water from their 660-gallon "Bambi buckets," while Chinooks with 2,000-gallon buckets added another half-million gallons to the total. Meanwhile, a host of helpers were hard at work behind the scenes, maintaining equipment, refueling, and filling water tanks; medical officers treated people for burns and the effects of heat exhaustion. Although given basic training in safety procedures, the guardsmen and -women made no claims to great firefighting experience or technical expertise. Florida National Guardsman Colonel Jimmy Watson was frank about how awesome he found the fire: "We're not professional firefighters," he freely admitted to *The News Hour with Jim Lehrer* reporter Phil Ponce:

"We have to have someone with us that knows exactly what they're doing. The times I've been up close to the fire it's almost like it's a living being, and you've got to know what you're doing because sometimes it'll be laying down, as they say, and then it's up, and it'll be on top of you. It'll travel 50 or a 100 yards (55–109 m) in just a matter of seconds."

Even when apparently extinguished, the fire could easily flare up again, hence the importance of "mop-up"—as crucial as "hot-line duty," the guards were told. As dry winds fanned

A Colorado National Guard helicopter carries a Bambi bucket in the effort to fight the Cold Springs Fire.

the flames ever higher, the guards continued to do their best, their capacity for disciplined collaboration more valuable than any specific skills in fighting fires. "They're easy to train," said Jim Harrington, a U.S. Forest Service fire manager flown in from Montana to help deal with the Florida fires. "They work hard for you. And they're structured." As is so often the case, the National Guard drew strength from the fact that it represented the community it was defending. Colonel Jimmy Watson was in no doubt of the significance of that fact: "As members of the affected communities ourselves, we have both a personal and professional interest in providing firefighting support." Hence the determination of another guardsman, Sergeant Kelvin Smith, who, despite his exhaustion, said, "I didn't know how hard it was going to be and how much they were going to push on us, but I am willing to do anything to get these fires under control." In the end, it took serious rainfall to put out the Florida fires once and for all, and with thousands of acres scorched, the results of the firefighting effort were not immediately apparent.

Yet, while 78 homes had been destroyed in the fire, many more had been successfully saved—and through all the drama not a single life had been lost.

Under Threat

Once, the threat to America came from Soviet tank battalions, bombers, and missiles. Now it could be anything from a car bomb to a bioweapon in a perfume bottle. In the space of the year 2015, no fewer than 383 million people passed through U.S. border controls, any one of whom could quite easily have been a terrorist. In addition, 103 million privately owned vehicles and 26.3 million truck, rail, and sea containers entered America—as did 112.5 million international air travelers and crew and 19.8 million passengers and crew arriving on ships. In 2000, of the 5,000 trucks a day that entered the country across Detroit's Ambassador Bridge, few could have been given more than the most cursory official inspection. American air carriers could boast by the end of 2015 that their planes had made possible 895 million individual international and domestic trips. How can America defend itself against the threat that lies hidden like a needle in a haystack—short, that is, of curbing its precious liberties or the free-flowing trade and commerce that are its economic lifeblood? The answer can only lie in greater levels of public education and public vigilance: the National Guard is working tirelessly to foster both. The National Guard is the lead military agent in Homeland Security, and the U.S. government continues to strengthen the Guard's funding and numbers to ensure maximum protection in times of crisis.

Mount St. Helens

In the rural east of Washington State, a spring Sunday morning dawned fine and clear. By noon on May 18, 1980, however, a fearful acrid rain was falling, draping the green fields and woods in a shroud of ghostly gray—ash vomited from the great volcano across the Cascade Mountains. The eruption of Mount St. Helens has gone down in geological history: its explosive eruption hurled ash and debris skyward with the force of a 24-megaton bomb. Anyone unfortunate enough to find themselves within five miles (8 km) of the mountain was effectively cooked on the spot, although even much farther afield, people died when exposed to its destructive force. The full force of the explosion blew sideways out through the mountainside, blasting to sterility a clear zone of several miles. It also sent ash spinning some 12 miles (19 km) into the air. In the weeks that followed, this was borne eastward by the wind, slowly coming to earth across the breadth of America, with traces falling on the shores of the Atlantic and, no doubt, beyond.

It was in Washington and the Pacific Northwest, however, that the effects were most strongly felt. The ashcloud blotted out the sun so completely that an apocalyptic darkness descended on the earth. Once they had overcome their initial shock, the people of these far-flung communities pulled together, their efforts led by members of the local National Guard. Setting up roadblocks to keep a safe cordon around the affected area, they organized an orderly evacuation of those at risk, while their helicopter pilots risked their lives to snatch stranded lumberjacks and backpackers from deep in the danger zone. "You know you have a job to perform in a very hostile environment," said Dick Latimer, a helicopter pilot who flew far too close to the volcano for anyone's comfort. Asked for his memories by a reporter from the Bremerton, WA, *Sun*, he added, "There is a feeling of repressed fear. It's not a Clint Eastwood kind of courage. You're looking at an atomic bomb explosion, and you know you have to fly into it."

One of a team of fliers with the National Guard's 116th Attack Troop, Latimer and his unit were on their annual training in nearby Yakima—just a short helicopter hop from the scene of the disaster. Sixteen helicopter crews joined with him in combing the slopes around Mount St. Helens, flying low along ridges in an effort to keep their bearings in all-but-impossible

A National Guard helicopter flies over Mount St. Helens.

conditions. So dense was the ash, he recalls, that the downwash of his rotors blotted out the Earth as he landed: "It was like shutting your eyes and jumping out of a swing," he recalled. Jess Hagerman, another National Guard helicopter pilot, admitted to "the worst case of vertigo I'd ever had," losing all sense of orientation as his helicopter wheeled and plunged in the white-out conditions of the swirling ashstorm. "The only response is to force yourself to believe the gauges. How we avoided the mountains that day I'll never know." Hagerman recalls yelling at one woman hillwalker he had rescued to toss her—surely unnecessary—backpack from his overburdened helicopter. "I've got my baby in there!" she indignantly replied.

With the courage of ordinary Americans like Dick Latimer and Jess Hagerman to call on, and many years' worth of experience and **accumulated** skills, the National Guard is uniquely

A National Guard for Israel?

Calls have been made in Israel for that country to have its own version of America's National Guard, specifically to coordinate the response to emergencies and natural disasters. With a five-decade history in which it has been almost continually at war with its Arab neighbors, Israel cannot be accused of being militarily unprepared. Civil-defense experts have, however, pointed to shortcomings in planning for major disasters, including earthquakes, noting the degree of duplication and inefficiency involved in the present arrangements. As of 2016, Israel's Home Front Command is the closest equivalent to the United States' National Guard. Founded in 1983, the Home Front Command is made up of reservists who are always on call to serve both domestically and abroad. The Command's first search and rescue company was formed in November 2003. The company is on call 24 hours a day and deploys when Israel experiences any kind of disaster, from earthquakes to terrorist attacks.

The Washington State National Guard responds to the Mt. St. Helens eruption.

qualified to lead the large-scale response to any disaster. And not only natural events, like floods, fires, and volcanoes: at one time or another, National Guard units have shown themselves able to deal with every type of humanmade disaster as well—everything from radioactive incidents and chemical spills to refugee crises. Ultimately, the National Guard's most precious resource is not any one specific technical capability, but its organizational abilities: discipline and loyalty are the keys to these. The never-say-die spirit of the men and women of the National Guard stems from their sense that they are friends and comrades working together for the protection of their own communities and their own country.

Text-Dependent Questions

1. How many troops did President Bush call into service following the events of September 11, 2001?
2. What was the National Guard's first task in fighting the fire that took place in Florida in 1998?
3. How did the National Guard help residents of Washington and the Pacific Northwest after Mount St. Helens erupted?

Research Projects

1. Research the Kiowa, Black Hawk, and Chinook helicopters used by the Air National Guard to combat the 1998 Florida fire. How many helicopters took part in the operation? What special equipment does each possess, and how was it used during the operation?
2. Research the Mt. St. Helens eruption. What was the extent of the lives lost and property destruction? How was the National Guard able to respond to this disaster?

CHAPTER 5

LOOKING FORWARD, REACHING OUT

Serving in the National Guard can build professional skills that serve recruits throughout their careers.

W e live, it seems, in increasingly dangerous times, in which our enemies are not always easy to identify, much less defend against. Easy travel and efficient tele-communications have made the world smaller than ever, with great benefits for all—but they have also brought us uncomfortably close to the world's many conflicts.

International terrorism can now no longer be dismissed as a concern for other countries; the trade in drugs has brought a host of evils to our own door. Global problems these may be, but their impact is felt on the streets of our cities and towns, where a **disaffected** "underclass" turns in desperation to drugs and crime. The mugger attacks America as surely as any missile; the drug dealer undermines the foundations of what should be a strong nation.

Might not both these "enemies," however, be victims in their turn? In recent years, in its efforts to reimagine what "guarding the nation" might actually mean in the 21st century, the National Guard has found itself tackling tough questions such as these. And it has concluded that the enlistment of young men and women in the defense of their own society will be central to the strength of America in the years to come.

Fighting for the Future

In America's impoverished inner cities, crime is very much a "real and present danger" in daily life, an enemy more frightening and destructive than any "rogue state" or terrorist organiza-tion. The National Guard must make an effort to guard against a foe that makes life miserable

Words to Understand

Disadvantaged: People living under unfavorable conditions, such as poverty.

Disaffected: Those dissatisfied with people in authority.

Interdiction: Disrupting or preventing.

Predatory: Those trying to oppress others.

Night vision technology is used by the National Guard to search for combatants.

for many thousands of U.S. citizens. Interpreting its mission more widely in recent years, the National Guard has made an invaluable contribution in the fight against crime, assisting law enforcement and other agencies in the **interdiction** of drug shipments and the arrest of criminals.

Its leadership has long felt, however, that the organization could contribute more. With its unique combination of community spirit and military discipline, the National Guard has something special to offer to the sort of young people who in the past have far too often drifted into crime. More than 10 million Americans a year drop out of school without gaining any qualifications—and, all too frequently, with very little in the way of "life skills." In 2012, the most recent data available, more than 12 million people were arrested nationwide, to be charged with a wide range of crimes, often violent and often drug related.

Using 2012 as an example, this means many thousands of crimes take place each year in every one of our states: the one thing they all have in common is that they are unnecessary. Young people who feel they have a future, and who feel some sense of involvement in society, do not want to lead the living-death existence of the drug addict, or the **predatory**, parasitical life of the shoplifter, street robber, or housebreaker. This is where the National Guard comes in, with its deep roots in every American community and its centuries-old tradition of fostering discipline and collective spirit. Its resources marshaled behind the banner of the imaginative ChalleNGe program, the National Guard has been making a major contribution to the creation of citizens, as well as the prevention of crime.

A Family Tradition

Scott Kyle, of Scottsville, NY, is in no doubt about why he signed up with the Army National Guard at the age of 19: "I'm a very patriotic person. One of the reasons I joined was to fight for my country." His country asks a lot of him; he told the New York *Catholic Courier* that on training weekends, "I bust my butt. But it's just a blast. I love it so far." Scott denies that his father—who saw action in the Vietnam War—made any attempt to sway him in his decision. He was grateful for his dad's unswerving support, however—while his father admits to feeling great pride in his son.

Alaska Military Youth ChalleNGe Academy cadets ceremoniously toss their berets in the air at their graduation.

Meeting the Challenge

Since its experimental inception in 1993, the National Guard Youth ChalleNGe program has made great strides, with 37 programs in 27 states participating—and several more preparing to start. More than 87 percent of those recruited so far have stayed with the program all the way to graduation; more than 15,000 young men and women to date have received their high school diploma or equivalent. The elderly and **disadvantaged** in our society have benefited too: ChalleNGe participants have contributed more than 24,000 hours of community service per year in ordinary American towns and city neighborhoods.

With experienced guardsmen and -women to act as mentors, ChalleNGe has the capacity to reach high school dropouts before they have been lost to society. It gives them the motivation and skills they need to make the most of the talents they have and to form a bond with society, which in many cases they have never

National Guard basic training—day one.

felt before. Assistance with academic work has already helped many thousands with GED/high school diploma attainments, which they might otherwise never have dreamt of obtaining, and this has opened up an enormous range of employment opportunities to those who once felt they had no choices. However, this is just the start of a program that is remarkably wide in its scope, extending to life-coping skills, community service, health and hygiene, skills training, leadership/followership, and physical training.

The aim of the program is to turn disaffected dropouts into proud and active American citizens, and, so far, the results have been highly encouraging. Skye Whaley is a 2008 graduate of Oregon's ChalleNGe program. She agreed to take part after she began smoking marijuana at the age of 15 and dropped out of high school. She says this about it, "Graduation day came and I couldn't be happier. I was giving a speech in honor of 4th Platoon, and I was graduating with a 3.4 GPA. . . . Thanks to everyone there, and some who are not there anymore, I graduated, and at the top of my class."

There is no doubt, however, that to meet the real challenges of the coming years, America will need to pull together to become a truly united society: the National Guard is leading the way to a stronger, happier future.

Text-Dependent Questions

1. Name one way the National Guard combats crime in the United States.
2. How many states participate in the ChalleNGe program?
3. Describe the overall aim of the ChalleNGe program.

Research Projects

1. Research one National Guard operation to combat crime. What is its mission, how many units are involved, and how successful has it been?
2. Research the ChalleNGe program. How many youths have successfully completed the program? How do the programs differ from state to state?

Series Glosssary

Air marshal: Armed guard traveling on an aircraft to protect the passengers and crew; the air marshal is often disguised as a passenger.

Annexation: To incorporate a country or other territory within the domain of a state.

Armory: A supply of arms for defense or attack.

Assassinate: To murder by sudden or secret attack, usually for impersonal reasons.

Ballistic: Of or relating to firearms.

Biological warfare: Also known as germ warfare, this is war fought with biotoxins—harmful bacteria or viruses that are artificially propagated and deliberately dispersed to spread sickness among an enemy.

Cartel: A combination of groups with a common action or goal.

Chemical warfare: The use of poisonous or corrosive substances to kill or incapacitate the enemy; it differs from biological warfare in that the chemicals concerned are not organic, living germs.

Cold War: A long and bitter enmity between the United States and the Free World and the Soviet Union and its Communist satellites, which went on from 1945 to the collapse of Communism in 1989.

Communism: A system of government in which a single authoritarian party controls state-owned means of production.

Conscription: Compulsory enrollment of persons especially for military service.

Consignment: A shipment of goods or weapons.

Contingency operations: Operations of a short duration and most often performed at short notice, such as dropping supplies into a combat zone.

Counterintelligence: Activities designed to collect information about enemy espionage and then to thwart it.

Covert operations: Secret plans and activities carried out by spies and their agencies.

Cyberterrorism: A form of terrorism that seeks to cause disruption by interfering with computer networks.

Democracy: A government elected to rule by the majority of a country's people.

Depleted uranium: One of the hardest known substances, it has most of its radioactivity removed before being used to make bullets.

Dissident: A person who disagrees with an established religious or political system, organization, or belief.

Embargo: A legal prohibition on commerce.

Emigration: To leave one country to move to another country.

Extortion: The act of obtaining money or other property from a person by means of force or intimidation.

Extradite: To surrender an alleged criminal from one state or nation to another having jurisdiction to try the charge.

Federalize/federalization: The process by which National Guard units, under state command in normal circumstances, are called up by the president in times of crisis to serve the federal government of the United States as a whole.

Genocide: The deliberate and systematic destruction of a racial, political, or cultural group.

Guerrilla: A person who engages in irregular warfare, especially as a member of an independent unit carrying out harassment and sabotage.

Hijack: To take unlawful control of a ship, train, aircraft, or other form of transport.

Immigration: The movement of a person or people ("immigrants") into a country; as opposed to emigration, their movement out.

Indict: To charge with a crime by the finding or presentment of a jury (as a grand jury) in due form of law.

Infiltrate: To penetrate an organization, like a terrorist network.

Infrastructure: The crucial networks of a nation, such as transportation and communication, and also including government organizations, factories, and schools.

Insertion: Getting into a place where hostages are being held.

Insurgent: A person who revolts against civil authority or an established government.

Internment: To hold someone, especially an immigrant, while his or her application for residence is being processed.

Logistics: The aspect of military science dealing with the procurement, maintenance, and transportation of military matériel, facilities, and personnel.

Matériel: Equipment, apparatus, and supplies used by an organization or institution.

Militant: Having a combative or aggressive attitude.

Militia: a military force raised from civilians, which supports a regular army in times of war.

Narcoterrorism: Outrages arranged by drug trafficking gangs to destabilize government, thus weakening law enforcement and creating conditions for the conduct of their illegal business.

NATO: North Atlantic Treaty Organization; an organization of North American and European countries formed in 1949 to protect one another against possible Soviet aggression.

Naturalization: The process by which a foreigner is officially "naturalized," or accepted as a U.S. citizen.

Nonstate actor: A terrorist who does not have official government support.

Ordnance: Military supplies, including weapons, ammunition, combat vehicles, and maintenance tools and equipment.

Refugee: A person forced to take refuge in a country not his or her own, displaced by war or political instability at home.

Rogue state: A country, such as Iraq or North Korea, that ignores the conventions and laws set by the international community; rogue states often pose a threat, either through direct military action or by harboring terrorists.

Sortie: One mission or attack by a single plane.

Sting: A plan implemented by undercover police in order to trap criminals.

Surveillance: To closely watch over and monitor situations; the USAF employs many different kinds of surveillance equipment and techniques in its role as an intelligence gatherer.

Truce: A suspension of fighting by agreement of opposing forces.

UN: United Nations; an international organization, of which the United States is a member, that was established in 1945 to promote international peace and security.

Chronology

1607: First militia companies are formed on English model by settlers in Jamestown, VA.

1636: Militia companies are organized into full-scale regiments by the General Court of the Massachusetts Bay Colony—the nearest thing England's North American colonies have to an elected "national" government.

1775: Battles of Lexington Green and Concord, precipitate the American Revolution.

1776: Benjamin Franklin, Thomas Jefferson, and others draw up the U.S. Declaration of Independence.

1781: Revolutionary War is brought to an end by the surrender of British forces under Lord Cornwallis—one of Europe's great armies is defeated by a militia force.

1789: George Washington becomes the first president of the United States.

1792: Uniform Militia Law makes service in militia mandatory for male citizens in the United States.

1824: Seventh Regiment of New York State Militia takes the title of "National Guard."

1848: Mexican War.

1861–1865: Civil War, in which militia forces fight on both sides.

1898: Spanish-American War, in which large numbers of Guardsmen fight—especially in the Philippines.

1903: Dick Act formally establishes the "National Guard" title and standardizes structure, organization, and equipment nationwide.

1914–1918: World War I, during which 18 National Guard divisions are sent to Europe.

1916: Defense Act formalizes system for federalization of state guards by the president in times of emergency; border conflict with Mexico.

1939–1945: World War II; U.S. forces are mobilized in 1940 and actively involved after the attack on Pearl Harbor in 1941; 19 National Guard divisions eventually fight in Europe and the Pacific.

1947: Formal establishment of the Air National Guard as a separate service.

1950–1953: Korean War.

1956: First woman, Norma Pearsons, appointed to serve in the National Guard.

1964–1974: Vietnam War.

1983: Invasion of Grenada.

1989: Operation Just Cause takes place in Panama.

1991: The Gulf War; in Operation Desert Storm, a U.S.-led coalition drives Saddam Hussein's Iraqi forces from Kuwait.

1993: Inauguration of ChalleNGe program for young people considered at risk of drifting into crime; experimental program established on a permanent basis, 1998.

2001: September 11 attacks; mass-mobilization of Army and Air National Guards, both central to civil-defense strategies of new Office of Homeland Security.

2002–2016: Operation Enduring Freedom, Afghanistan.

2003–2011: Operation Iraqi Freedom.

2005: Search and rescue, protection, etc., after Hurricane Katrina.

2016: Spc. Rachel Mayhew becomes Texas Army Guard's first female combat engineer.

Further Resources

Websites

The official website of the U.S. National Guard: www.ngb.dtic.mil

For current National Guard-related news stories, see the U.S. Army's own online news service: www.dtic.mil/armylink

For background information, see: www.military.com

For information about the National Guard's Youth Foundation, see: www.ngyf.org

Air National Guard: www.ang.af.mil/index.asp

Further Reading

Berebitsky, William. *A Very Long Weekend: The Army National Guard in Korea, 1950–1953*. Shippensberg, PA: White Mane, 2001.

Doubler, Col. Michael D. *I Am the Guard: A History of the Army National Guard, 1636–2000*. Washington, D.C.: Government Printing Office, 2002.

Flynn, Sean Michael. *The Fighting 69th: From Ground Zero to Baghdad*. New York, NY: Viking Penguin, 2008.

Gross, Dr. Charles J. *From Shield to Storm: The Air National Guard and the Persian Gulf Crisis*. Collingdale, PA: DIANE, 1994.

Gross, Dr. Charles J. *The Air National Guard: A Short History*. Washington, D.C.: Government Printing Office, 1994.

Kelly, Terrence K. "Transformation and Homeland Security: Dual Challenges for the US Army," *Parameters*, Vol. 33, No. 2, Summer 2003.

Spencer, Jack. *The Role of the National Guard in Homeland Security*. Washington, D.C.: The Heritage Foundation, 2002.

North Carolina National Guard Tarheel Challenge Cadets train at Camp Butner in Stem, NC. The training is part of a program for at-risk youth, who volunteer to participate.

Index

About the Author

Michael Kerrigan was born in Liverpool, England, and educated at St. Edward's College, from where he won an Open Scholarship to University College, Oxford. He lived for a time in the United States, spending time first at Princeton University, followed by a period working in publishing in New York. Since then he has been a freelance writer and journalist, with commissions across a wide range of subjects, but with a special interest in social policy and defense issues. Within this field, he has written on every region of the world. His work has been published by a number of leading international educational publishers, including the BBC, Dorling Kindersley, Time-Life, and Reader's Digest Books. His work as a journalist includes regular contributions to the *Times Literary Supplement*, London, as well as a weekly column in the *Scotsman* newspaper, Edinburgh, where he now lives with his wife and their two small children.

About the Consultant

Manny Gomez, an expert on terrorism and security, is President of MG Security Services and a former Principal Relief Supervisor and Special Agent with the FBI. He investigated terrorism and espionage cases as an agent in the National Security Division. He was a certified undercover agent and successfully completed Agent Survival School. Chairman of the Board of the National Law Enforcement Association (NLEA), Manny is also a former Sergeant in the New York Police Department (NYPD) where he supervised patrol and investigative activities of numerous police officers, detectives and civilian personnel. Mr. Gomez worked as a uniformed and plainclothes officer in combating narcotics trafficking, violent crimes, and quality of life concerns. He has executed over 100 arrests and received Departmental recognition on eight separate occasions. Mr. Gomez has a Bachelor's Degree and Master's Degree and is a graduate of Fordham University School of Law where he was on the Dean's list. He is admitted to the New York and New Jersey Bar. He served honorably in the United States Marine Corps infantry.